Skateboarding Skills

Skateboarding Skills

THE RIDER'S GUIDE

BEN POWELL

FIREFLY BOOKS

A FIREFLY BOOK

Published by Firefly Books Ltd. 2008

Copyright © 2008 Axis Publishing Ltd.

First printing

Publisher Cataloging-in-Publication Data (U.S.)
Powell, Ben.
     Skateboarding skills : the rider's guide / Ben Powell.
[128] p. : col. photos. ;   cm.
Includes index.
Summary: Skateboarding techniques from beginner to advanced are covered, along with equipment and expert tips. Moves are broken down into their component parts, with picture sequences and captions.
ISBN-13: 978-1-55407-360-3
ISBN-10: 1-55407-360-X
1. Skateboarding. I. Title.
796.22 dc22   GV859.8.P6955 2008

Library and Archives Canada Cataloguing in Publication
Powell, Ben
     Skateboarding skills : the rider's guide / Ben Powell.
Includes index.
ISBN-13: 978-1-55407-360-3
ISBN-10: 1-55407-360-X
     1. Skateboarding—Juvenile literature. I. Title.
GV859.8.P693 2008   j796.22   C2007-905509-5

Published in the United States in 2008 by
Firefly Books (U.S.) Inc.
P.O. Box 1338, Ellicott Station
Buffalo, New York 14205

Published in Canada in 2008 by
Firefly Books Ltd.
66 Leek Crescent
Richmond Hill, Ontario L4B 1H1

Conceived and created by
Axis Publishing Limited
www.axispublishing.co.uk

Creative Director: Siân Keogh
Production Manager: Jo Ryan

Cover Design: Erin R. Holmes

Printed in China

Skateboarding is an activity with a danger of personal injury, particularly if engaged in without proper safety gear. Participants in this activity should be aware of and accept these risks and accept responsibility for their own actions. Always use good judgment based on a realistic assessment of your own skills and limitations.

contents

introduction

Skateboarding is everything and nothing. It can become your whole life, or it can be nothing more significant than a cheap and enjoyable form of transport. It all depends on the limits of your imagination.

You might imagine that you already know what skateboarding is when you pick up this book. You have seen professional skateboarding on mainstream television and have witnessed the tricks that can be performed on a skateboard; you may even have played a computer game that promises to reveal the secrets of skateboarding to the uninitiated. No matter where you first encountered the ubiquitous wooden plank on wheels, only one thing is certain: without the experience of actually riding a skateboard down a busy street, or threading your path through the crowds and traffic while surrounded by the noises of the city, you have absolutely no idea what it means to be a skateboarder.

HISTORY

Skateboards were first recorded in the mid-1950s and originated from California's warm beach towns. The earliest skateboards would seem extremely primitive to today's skaters. These rudimentary boards were really the ramshackle offspring of a marriage between boxcar racers and crude dry-land surfboards. The boards were much smaller than their modern counterparts: the trucks did not have the capacity to turn, and the wheels were one-piece affairs made from either clay or metal. Although the basic principle of "traveling without moving," which underlies skateboarding to this day, was evident in these early boards, the ride was much more limited and basic than that enjoyed by modern skaters with state-of-the-art boards.

Early bands of skateboarders were only found in a handful of surf communities in the United States until the 1970s, when several toy manufacturers discovered the emerging "skateboard craze" and started to mass-manufacture skateboards for the first time. Interest in skateboarding boomed in the mid-1970s as the media began to report on this new sport, and photographs of

6

skateboarders started to appear in advertisements and newspapers across the world. As the boom set in, custom-built skateparks began to spring up in cities and towns to meet the needs of the skateboarders by providing monitored replicas of the banks and slopes of the streets in a controlled environment.

Skateboarding quickly became a massively profitable business, and with that came all the trappings of popularity—competitions, champions, professionals and various endorsed products. In just two decades, skateboarding had leapt in status from a homemade hobby to a semi-legitimate sport; it looked set to take the entire world by storm. Unfortunately, the profit-driven direction of the early boom also served to provide the stage for the great crash that befell skateboarding at the end of the 1970s. Badly designed skateparks and inadequate safety equipment led to a wave of lawsuits and park closures. By 1980 (only five years after the great boom), skateboarding was officially declared dead.

BACK TO ITS ROOTS

In truth, skateboarding did not die. The remaining groups of committed skaters moved out of the spotlight and back to the streets and backyard pools from which they had originally emerged. As most major sports manufacturers stopped making skateboards after the boom ended, skaters were forced to start small companies and set about making their own equipment. Innovations in the design of basic skateboard components

came to light during this period, as skateboarders themselves began improving performance to enhance their own participation in the sport. Along with these technical innovations came a decade of exploration and invention in terms of the ways that the skateboard could be manipulated by the skater. Most of the tricks featured in this book were invented during this underground period of skateboarding's history, from the mid-1980s to the latter part of the 1990s.

Ironically, the great crash served to concentrate small pockets of hard-core skaters and gave them the freedom to discover the potential of skateboarding. Freed from the conventions of custom-built environments and competition, skateboarding became the amorphous, shifting sub-culture that it is today, and not the clean cut "sport" envisaged by the entrepreneurs of the first boom.

And so we arrive at the present day. Skateboarding is everywhere and has finally regained the levels of exposure and popularity that it last enjoyed for a brief moment in the mid-1970s. Skateboarding may be new to you, but behind it lies a long and complex history, albeit one that is largely undocumented outside of specialist magazines. The experiences of this history have created skateboarding as it stands today: neither a sport nor a pastime, neither an art form nor a child's game, but an activity with millions of participants that is liberated from any rules and regulations. Skateboarding just is: all you have to do is get on one and roll. It makes much more sense then. Just enjoy it.

chapter one

get on your board

Before we talk about the technicalities, equipment and how to master a few tricks, we want you to be inspired. We want you to see what's out there and take your boarding to the next level. We will bring you up-to-date with skateboard history and legend. We will introduce you to the best skate parks in the world and, we hope, make you want to get on your board and get out there. We show you what you will find, from ramps to street courses, and outline skateboarding etiquette so you don't alienate other skaters. And we tell you about sponsorship—in case you're any good.

in the beginning	10
concrete skateparks	12
indoor wooden parks	14
skate plazas	16
skateboarding events	20
sponsorship	22

in the beginning

The now global phenomenon that is skateboarding began as nothing more than a dry-land alternative to surfing, invented as a way for surfers to pass the time when the waves were flat.

In the beginning, skateboarding was nothing more than a mode of transport perfectly suited to the smooth cement streets of California. There were no tricks, no skateparks, no pros; nothing we associate with skateboarding today.

For a decade or so skateboarding lay dormant, until the original skateboard boom of the mid 1970s took hold, and skateboard parks were built to cater to this new hobby that was taking over the world. Toward the end of this boom, a group of skaters from the Santa Monica area of California came to prominence within the skateboarding world due to the type of skateboarding they were doing. This group of skaters went on to radically alter everything about skate culture and became the sport's first ever skateboarding superstars. Where the first generation of professionals had competed against each other in the now long-dead disciplines of skateboarding long-jump, high-jump and slalom, Tony Alva, Stacey Peralta, Jay Adams and the rest of the Dogtown scene were pushing skateboarding in a more aggressive and radical direction.

Alva, Adams and company dispensed with the score sheets and team outfits of their contemporaries and pushed skateboarding to a whole new level, outside the monitored confines of the public skateparks of the times. Instead, they opted to search out backyard swimming pools to perfect their art.

10

concrete skateparks

Concrete parks were the original custom-made skateboard facilities, and hundreds of thousands of them were built during the 1970s skateboard craze.

When skateboarding took a nosedive in the mid-1980s, all but a few of the epic 70s skateparks were demolished. The ones that remained became the proving ground for the dwindling numbers of remaining hard-core skaters. Due to the costs involved, new concrete parks were a rarity until the end of the 1990s, when skateboarding's popularity surged again. Nowadays, the best skateparks in the world are concrete, and all clued-in skaters lust after one in their hometown.

From the very beginning, the second wave of concrete park construction has been led by skateboarders with skater-owned companies, such as Oregon's "Dreamland" and "Grindline," building seemingly impossible dreamscapes, incorporating aspects of every side of skateboarding and sculpted to perfection.

1 Concrete parks are favored by skaters because they are the fastest and most gnarly of all skateparks. Concrete parks always emphasize "lines." This layout allows the skater to lead each trick right into the next while maintaining high speeds.

2 Most traditional concrete skateparks concentrate on flowing designs that incorporate curves, steep, transitions and bowls, rather than smaller, more technical obstacles.

3 Concrete parks often have concrete or "pool" coping, which harkens back to the original pool-skating era. Skaters agree that concrete coping gives the most satisfying grind against the board.

4 Some of the world's most famous concrete skateparks include: Burnside in Oregon; Livingston, better known as Livi in Scotland; Kona in Florida; Marseille, or Marsy, in France; Stapelbaddsparken in Malmo, Sweden; and the unbelievable SMP super-park in Shanghai, China.

SKATEPARK OBSTACLES

BOWLS
Bowls are one of oldest of all skatepark obstacles. Bowl skating was the most popular form of skating in the 1970s, and the fundamentals of many tricks were first invented in bowls.

SNAKE RUNS
The curving, twisted ride of the snake run was a staple of all original concrete skateparks. As tricks and styles of skateboarding evolved away from surfing, snake runs became less popular.

BANKED SLALOM RUNS
When the first skateparks were being constructed, downhill slalom was still a major discipline. The runs would be downhill, with curved or banked walls running all the way along the run on both sides. As skateboarding progressed, slalom runs evolved into the modern half-pipe to cater to a new, trick-heavy style.

By virtue of being constructed in concrete and, usually, of epic scale, concrete parks like the ones mentioned can be dangerous places for beginners. In large-scale parks, safety clothing is advisable, as well as taking the time to work out which areas are the safest for beginners and which aren't.

13

indoor wooden parks

The indoor wooden park owes its existence to the period in the 1980s when skateboarding was virtually dead as far as the outside world was concerned. As the major concrete parks were demolished, the skaters that remained were faced with two options; either build their own ramps or quit.

This situation led to the 1980s "backyard ramp" phenomenon, and the subsequent invention of the modern half-pipe. The wooden park was a lot cheaper and easier to build for the regular skater, so throughout the 1980s people experimented with all manner of obstacle ideas, bringing us up to the present day where most ramps have various additions first conceived of in the era when skateboarding was dead.

Wooden parks are often the only option for skaters who live in countries with wet winter weather. As such, they are a lifeline for skaters the world over. Today, the limitations as to what can be done with wooden skateparks have been shattered, and most major cities will

have a least one good indoor park. Wooden parks are excellent places for beginners. The wooden surface is much more forgiving than concrete, and most indoor parks will have a specific beginner section with scaled-down versions of the main obstacles. Most wooden skateparks will contain a combination of transitioned or ramp-based obstacles, as well as more street-oriented fixtures. Most layouts will include some of the following: vert ramp, mini-ramp, bowl, street course, ledges, spines, rails and more. Indoor parks also tend to be the sites for most grassroots skate events, and thus provide the perfect place to meet new friends and get yourself known on the scene.

WOODEN SKATEPARK OBSTACLES

VERT RAMP
Generally constructed from wood, the vert ramp is the gnarliest thing in the skatepark. Averaging at least 11 feet (3 m) high, with anything from 6 inches (10 cm) to 2 feet (.6 m) of sheer vertical, the vert ramp is the fastest and most exhilarating ride you'll get.

FUNBOX
Any good wooden skatepark will house a funbox of some description. A funbox is any variation of a simple theme: a four-sided square platform with ramps on each side. There are an infinite number of possible variations on this basic idea.

MINI
This is basically a scaled down version of the vert ramp. Mini-ramps are a perfect place for learning —whether you're a beginner or an advanced skater, the mellower transitions of the mini-ramp will allow you to experiment in a way that bigger obstacles do not.

STREET COURSE
The most popular area in most wooden skateparks will be the street course. There are many possibilities, but most street courses will contain at least some of these obstacles: ledges, hips, manual pads, driveways and more besides.

Famous indoor skateparks include: Skatepark of Tampa, Florida; Radlands, Northampton, U.K.; Mystic Skate Park, Prague, Czech Republic; and many more.

skate plazas

Skate plazas are a relatively new development in the history of skatepark construction. Unlike most concrete or wood parks, plaza-style skateparks attempt to recreate real street environments based on famous street spots from across the world.

One of the first skate plazas to be built was the Rob Dyrdek Plaza in Kettering, Ohio, which was campaigned for, and designed by, pro skater and MTV star Rob Dyrdek. The Kettering plaza focused on real street obstacles specifically constructed and placed to maximize their skateability and has since set a precedent that has been repeated all over the world.

The popularity of skate plazas has grown hugely over the last few years, as widespread clampdowns on street skating have become the norm, particularly in the United States. In the face of anti-skate legislation and architectural modifications to render street spaces less amenable to skateboarders, plazas provide a safe and legal alternative.

Skate plazas take their inspiration from famous street spots that have since been demolished or rendered off-limits by security guards or skate-stoppers. The famous "Love Park" spot in Philadelphia is one such example. The local authorities banned skateboarding there, so skate plaza designers across the globe copied aspects of the space and recreated it elsewhere.

Plazas tend to be filled with real street obstacles, some of which can be dangerous to the beginner. Stay away from steps and handrails to begin with, and use the smooth, flat ground that all skate plazas have in abundance. This is a perfect place to learn the basics of board control.

Remember that in a plaza everything is potentially skateable, so be wary of sitting on anything—it may look like a bench, but it's more likely to be the middle of somebody's line. Keep your wits about you.

Skate plazas are often popular for skate demonstrations and tour stop-offs, so they're also a great place to see professional skaters tearing it up.

As plaza layouts are often based on real street environments, you may often find yourself skating a replica of a set of stairs or a handrail from a city thousands of miles away from you. Some of the most replicated plaza spots follow.

THE PIER 7 BLOCK:
Nearly every plaza ever built has one of these. The original Pier 7 skate spot was situated in San Francisco and was recently skate-stopped and rendered off limits by the San Francisco Police Department. This obstacle is a square ledge with a low end (around 6 inches [15 cm] high) and a higher end to drop off. Pier 7 ledges are a place where extremely complex technical tricks are performed.

THE BIG 4:
The Big 4 obstacle originated in Barcelona, Spain, and the many variations on the theme are based on a real set of stairs outside the MACBA art gallery. Rather than small foot-step sized steps, your typical Big 4 has chunkier, amphitheater steps. The original MACBA Big 4 has become a proving ground for technical skaters all over the world and has appeared on every major skate video in the last five years.

THE HUBBA:
This is another famous San Franciscan skate spot that has been replicated in skate plazas and skateparks across the world. A Hubba is a solid slab version of a handrail down stairs. The original Hubba rose to legendary status because of its appearance in many influential skate videos and the many groundbreaking tricks done there for the first time.

skateboarding events

Events are the cement that holds any skateboard scene together. A skate event can be anything from a mass media event with live television and hundreds of pros right down to local events put on by skaters for skaters.

Until you venture out of your own local scene into the wider world, you will only see one side of skateboarding and your experience will be incomplete. Consult your local skate magazine or the Internet for more information; there are events happening all over the world that you can get involved with.

Skate events can take many forms—some will be serious affairs with regimented judging, timed runs and a heavy emphasis on competition, while others could be more jam-based affairs where the event is really nothing more than an excuse for a bunch of skaters to get together and have fun.

Many of you will have seen skateboard competitions such as the X Games on television—these are mainstream media events that attract some of the world's top pros. Unfortunately, they also attract hordes of non-skate media who don't always understand skate culture and whose coverage can make the scene look cheesy and mainstream.

Local or grassroots events are usually most skater's introduction to the wider scene. They will focus more on fun and inclusion than your average serious contest. Everyone is welcome, so get involved.

Skate events are a perfect place to experience what is really meant by the term "skate session": outside of skate comps and events, it is unlikely that you would get the opportunity to skate with hundreds of people at once. There is no feeling like being involved in a heavy session at a skate contest: dozens of people hitting the same obstacle, the excitement pushing the skating beyond normal levels and the atmosphere. You must experience it to understand it.

ETIQUETTE

Once you get to the stage where you are ready to enter local contests there are a few important rules to remember:

Nobody likes a "comper." Comping is used as a description for skaters who deliberately try to humiliate their opponents by doing the same tricks and then staring them down.

Nobody likes a big head—if you skate well then be happy. Do not roll around cheering for yourself like an idiot. Many a skate career has been ruined by this kind of behavior. Be happy but humble.

It's okay to be enthuastic and excited, to shout, to cheer, to smack your board against the coping in response to somebody going off. Skateboarding is about having fun, so leave your headphones and your attitude at home.

Concentrate on being well rounded as a skater, rather than focusing on one particular style of skateboarding. Being able to rip on all terrains will pay dividends if you decide that the contest circuit is for you.

sponsorship

For many people, sponsorship is the holy grail of skateboarding. Being sponsored can mean various things, depending on the level of sponsorship. It should be looked at as an amazing opportunity, rather than just a chance to score a load of free gear.

At its most basic level, sponsorship means that skaters are sent free products—boards, shoes, clothing, etc.—so that the skater can represent the brands in photos and videos. There are three basic modes of skateboard sponsorship:

FLOW

This is usually the entry point for any skater on the way up. Being part of a flow program means that although you may not officially be on the team or be featured in advertisements, your skills and attitude have been recognized. Flow sponsorship is usually the route into real team sponsorship, so while you are "on flow" you're expected to attend every event you can and shoot photos for skate magazines.

AMATEUR

This is the next step up from flow sponsorship. Once you're an amateur on a team you will be included in advertising, tours and videos, and you are in a position where you need to work hard and represent your sponsors. Most amateurs are unpaid but receive plenty of products, as well as "photo incentives" for every photo used where the sponsor's logos are visible.

PRO

At this stage, skateboarding is a full-time job with all the responsibilities, obligations and expectations that the title "pro skater" suggests. There are only a small number of truly legitimate pro skaters in the world, who continually push skateboarding and its progression, and who travel the world to promote the activity. The top level of pro skaters can earn huge salaries but be warned: nothing in life is free, and all pro skaters work extremely hard, often embarking on international tours that last months at a time.

chapter two

equipment

Skateboards have changed a lot since they first appeared in the 1950s. Here is all the technical information you need to know to choose the right board for you and get the best performance out of it. We show you what to look for in the deck, trucks and wheels. We also cover the latest footwear and safety gear. When buying a board for the first time you need to know your stance: are you regular or goofy? So we show you how to work it out. Then you are ready to go.

skateboard anatomy	**26**
decks	**28**
skateboard trucks	**32**
skateboard wheels	**34**
skateboard footwear	**36**
stances	**38**
safety equipment	**40**

skateboard anatomy

The basic makeup of the skateboard has hardly changed in the last 30 years. Individual components have been refined and updated, but the four fundamentals of board, trucks, wheels and bearings have remained constant throughout.

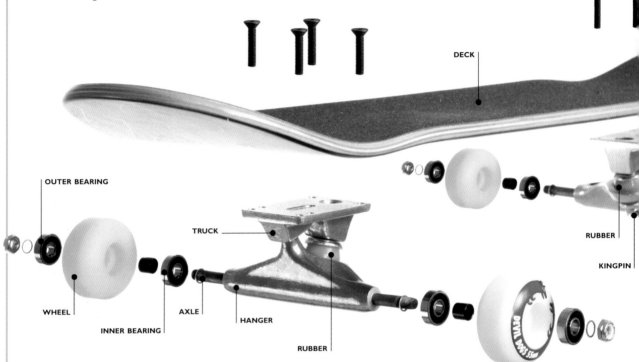

OUTER BEARING

DECK

TRUCK

RUBBER

KINGPIN

WHEEL

AXLE

HANGER

INNER BEARING

RUBBER

SKATEBOARD, OR DECK

Most skateboards are made from laminated sheets of plywood, using epoxy resins to cement the layers together. The kicktails and concave of the board are produced using molds at skateboard factories. Most modern skateboards are about 31 inches (78 cm) long and between 7 and 8 inches (18 and 20 cm) wide. Most of them will be fairly symmetrical in shape, with nose and kicktails to facilitate regular- and switch-skating.

WHEELS

Skateboard wheels are made from polyurethane and come in various diameters and hardness readings. Soft wheels give more grip, whereas hard wheels slide more easily on the ground and allow skaters to slide from one direction to another at will. Most street wheels will be between 90 a and 110 a (hardness) on the durometer (see page 34), with slalom or downhill wheels coming in at a softer 65 a to 85 a.

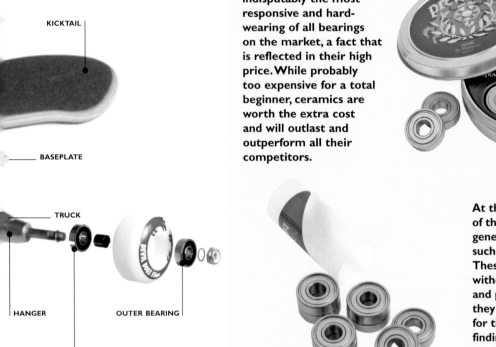

KICKTAIL

BASEPLATE

TRUCK

HANGER

OUTER BEARING

INNER BEARING

BEARINGS

Although less exciting looking than the rest of your set up, bearings are the most important part of your skateboard, as they are what allow you to roll.

Ceramic bearings are indisputably the most responsive and hard-wearing of all bearings on the market, a fact that is reflected in their high price. While probably too expensive for a total beginner, ceramics are worth the extra cost and will outlast and outperform all their competitors.

At the beginner's end of the market are the generic bearing brands, such as NMBs and SKF. These bearings come without flashy packaging and pro-endorsement, but they will work perfectly for those of you just finding your feet in the world of skateboarding.

TRUCKS

These are the metal axles to which the wheels are attached and that allow the skateboard to be turned while moving. Trucks are comprised of four elements.

■ HANGERS

The metal grinding edge that houses the axle to which the wheels are attached.

■ BASEPLATE

The metal seat that houses the hanger.

■ KINGPIN

Threaded bar that holds the hanger in the baseplate.

■ RUBBERS

Urethane grommets that surround the kingpin and allow the board to turn from side to side.

decks

The size and shape of the average skateboard deck has changed as the art of skateboarding itself has progressed and evolved. Types of decks relate directly to specific eras and to the styles of skating that were being performed. Over the last four decades there have been five major shifts in standard deck design.

THE EARLY 1970s

In the earliest days of skateboarding, all decks were scaled-down versions of the classic surfboard shape. At this time, skaters really only used their skateboards to carve around and imitate the movements of surfers.

THE LATE 1970s

It was at this stage that the kicktail was first introduced. It is now a standard feature of skateboard decks. The kicktail allowed skaters to perform kickturns and begin to develop tricks. At this point, most decks were still a lot shorter and narrower than today.

THE 1980s

The development of tricks in the 80s and the focus on skating big transitions and vert ramps laid the way for the next big development in deck design: the "fishtail" board. These boards were much wider and longer than their predecessors, generally around 32 inches long by 10 inches wide, (1 m by 25 cm) and had huge flared-out kicktails, which were perfectly suited for vertical skating.

THE 1990s

During this era the template for the majority of today's board shapes was created. The 90s saw the rise of a much more technical form of street skating and the establishment of "switch stance" skating, which meant that skaters used both stances to explore their range of tricks further than ever before. This evolution led to the development of the double-kick or "popsicle" deck shape, which has kicktails on both the nose and the tail to facilitate modern street tricks.

PRESENT DAY

The popsicle shape established in the early 90s still holds today, with minor adjustments in width and construction, and it looks set to remain the predominant deck type for some time to come.

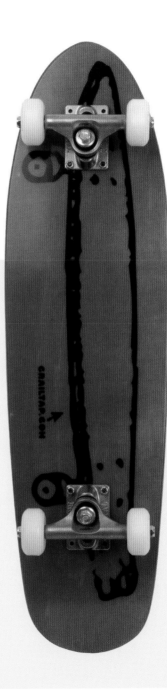

STANDARD DECK SHAPES TODAY

Most street and park decks will have roughly the same symmetrical, double-ended shape and generally are about 30 × 8 inches (1 m × 20 cm).

VERT BOARDS:

tend to be slightly larger than average to help with stability at the high speeds involved in skating vert ramps. The average vert board these days will have a slightly longer wheelbase (the space between the truck holes) and will usually be slightly wider than a street deck. Vert boards have amazing graphics, as these examples show.

SLALOM BOARDS:

have changed little over the last 30 years. Slalom boards are often shorter, thinner and lighter than average decks to allow the skater to be able to turn more quickly. This helps them to weave in and out of slalom cones. The average slalom board is around 30 inches (1 m) long by anywhere between 6–9 inches (15–23 cm) wide. Slalom boards tend not to have kicktails, as slalom riders turn by carving from side to side.

LONGBOARDS:
have always been a big part of skateboarding, even though they tend not to feature heavily in the mainstream skate media. As the name suggests, longboards are a lot bigger than your average deck. They help skaters deal with the speeds involved in downhill skating. The average longboard will be at least 40 inches (1.2 m) long and a little wider than an average board.

COLLECTOR'S BOARDS:
are at the top end of the market and are often bought without the skater having any intention of ever riding it. Collectors can pay huge amounts for original, pristine 70s and 80s boards, but stock is limited, so many companies have started to reissue classic deck shapes and graphics to cater to this growing market.

31

skateboard trucks

Skateboard trucks have changed very little in the last 15 years or so, as the classic truck design is as near to perfect as can be.

Of the three or so major brands available, most are very similar, with any differences usually being fairly minor and relating to specific types of skateboarding. The major things to look out for when choosing trucks are weight, hangar width and responsiveness to turning.

Independent—Indy has been the leading truck brand since the early 80s. It is the truck of choice for a vast majority of skateboarders because of the consistency of its grind and its fast turning response. Indy produces trucks with hangar lengths from 5–8 inches (13–20 cm), with the wider, heavier trucks being the most popular choice with vert and pool riders.

INDEPENDENT STAGE 9 FRONT VIEW

INDEPENDENT KOSTON LOW FRONT VIEW

INDEPENDENT STAGE 9 REAR VIEW

INDEPENDENT KOSTON LOW REAR VIEW

Venture—This is a long-established San Franciscan truck company. It rose to prominence alongside the development of street skating in the late 1980s. Venture trucks tend to be a lot lighter than Indy's and have baseplates with cut-out sections to make them even lighter, which helps to reduce the board weight.

Thunder—Another San Franciscan brand, Thunder trucks are similar in weight and size to Venture's and come in a variety of colors and professionally endorsed variations. Thunder's are often the truck of choice for the burlier street skater who also dabbles with park and ramp skating. They come in high and low heights and are one of the lightest trucks.

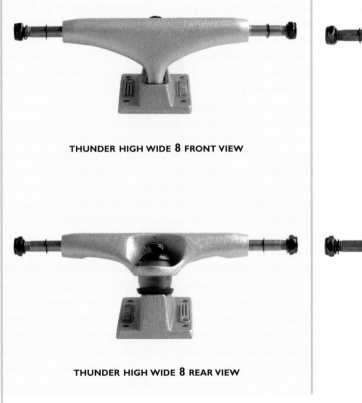

THUNDER HIGH WIDE 8 FRONT VIEW

THUNDER JENSEN PRO LOW FRONT VIEW

THUNDER HIGH WIDE 8 REAR VIEW

THUNDER JENSEN PRO LOW REAR VIEW

skateboard wheels

Since the introduction of the polyurethane skateboard wheel into the market in the late 1970s (invented by skater/engineer Frank Nasworthy), little has changed as far as wheel design goes. The main advancement has been in variations in diameter and durometer reading (i.e. wheel hardness). The harder a wheel is, or the

higher its durometer reading, the easier it is to slide the wheels across a concrete surface.

The standard durometer reading for most street or park skate wheels will be between the 98 a to 100 a mark on the durometer. For downhill, slalom or speed wheels, the durometer reading will be much lower

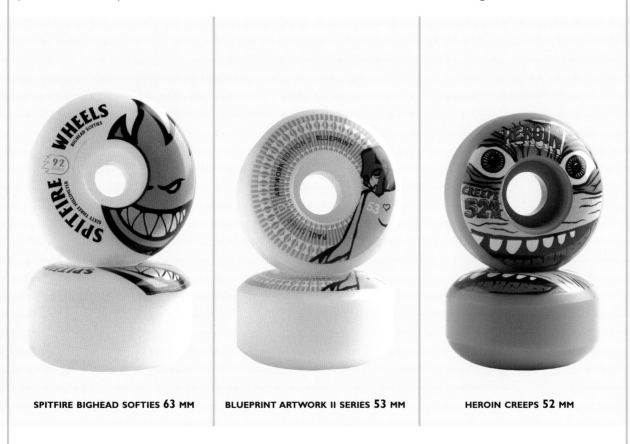

SPITFIRE BIGHEAD SOFTIES 63 MM   **BLUEPRINT ARTWORK II SERIES 53 MM**   **HEROIN CREEPS 52 MM**

(around 70 a–85 a), as the softer wheels provide much more grip at high speed.

Typical wheel sizes for most skaters these days will be ¼–½ inch or 50–60 mm (wheel sizes are almost invariably in millimeters). Wheel size should relate to the kind of surfaces and obstacles that you intend to skate.

The smaller end of the wheel market is suited toward more technical street skating. The 60mm and above ranges are aimed more squarely at pool and vert riders.

There are a huge number of skate wheels available, so your best bet is to talk to your local skate store to see what will work best for you.

BLUEPRINT BAINES 50 MM   LANDSCAPE SNOWY 52 MM   BONES SOFTCORE 52 MM

skateboard footwear

There are three basic requirements of skateboard footwear: flat, grippy soles; reinforced uppers to cope with the abuse that everyday skateboarding will mete out; and cushioning and support to absorb the impact involved in modern skateboarding.

With so many brands on the market, there are countless variations on these three necessities, and each skater will prefer a different type of shoe for the "feel" or look it gives. Popular brands include the following.

Vans—For many skaters, Vans are the original skateboard-specific shoe and thus they are the obvious choice. Vans pioneered the waffle sole, which is universally agreed to be the most grippy skateboard sole of all time. The most popular Vans shoe of the moment is probably the Geoff Rowley pro shoe; a beefed-up amalgam of many classic Vans shoes, complete with waffle sole and heel cushioning to absorb impact.

Emerica—Emerica, part of the Sole-Technologies brand, are hugely popular among street skaters. They offer unparalleled grip and technical cushioning techniques. As street skating moved toward bigger drops, stairs and rails, Sole Technology invested heavily in research and development to cater specifically to the bruised heels of modern skaters. Their STI system adds foam cushioning to every part of the sole to better absorb impact. The most popular Emerica shoe of the moment is undoubtedly the Andrew Reynolds model, with triple-stitched uppers and STI heel technology.

Lakai—Like Emerica, Lakai is a skater-owned shoe

brand. The emphasis is on both the look and the performance of the shoe. Lakai produce a range of skate-specfic shoes, with the most popular being their slimline vulcanized range, including models such as the Howard Select and the Manchester. Lakai prides itself on offering protection while retaining the feel of the board through the soles. They may feel a little less robust than some of their counterparts, but they work very well unless you're planning to launch yourself down 30 stairs.

Globe—This Australian brand started off small but has risen to prominence over the last five years. This is due to innovations in construction and the publicity from their amazing team riders. Globe offer vulcanized skate shoes with additional heel cushioning, as well as more technical models. The most popular of Globe's range at present is the Mark Appleyard model. It combines fashion upper stylings with performance stitching and cushioned soles.

Fallen—owned by infamous pro skater Jamie Thomas, Fallen aim their shoes squarely at the more aggressive end of street skating. They have additional heel cushioning and triple-stitched uppers. Their look tends to be a lot simpler than many of their competitors, with an emphasis on strong branding and simple, uncluttered upper designs. The most popular model at present is the Jamie Thomas "Chief" model.

stances

There are two types of stance in skateboarding: regular-footed and goofy-footed. These are terms that originate from surfing and relate to the foot that you lead with while skating.

Regular-footers ride with their left foot at the front of their boards; goofy-footers stand with their right foot forward. One stance will feel more natural than the other, as nature seems to attribute a stance in the same way that some people are left-handed and others are right-handed.

FRONTSIDE AND BACKSIDE

As with the names of the stances, frontside and backside are surf-derived terms to describe the direction of movement of skaters. Frontside means any trick or movement where skaters face their direction of travel. Backside refers to any trick or movement where skaters face away from their direction of travel.

To comprehend these two terms, it helps to imagine that you are a surfer on a wave. If you turn at the crest facing into the wave, then you are turning in a frontside direction. If you turn with your back facing the crest of the wave, then the direction is described as backside.

REGULAR

GOOFY

SWITCHSTANCE

One of the most unique innovations within skateboarding was the introduction of the idea that skaters could fully master their "unnatural" stance, so as to be able to skate equally well with either foot leading. The concept of switch-skating did not exist until the early 1990s. Various professional street skaters of the day (Mark Gonzales, Natas Kaupas, Mike Carrol and Henry Sanchez among many others) decided to reinvent skateboarding by announcing on their high-profile skate videos that it was good to learn to skate both ways.

Switchstance is one example of the fundamental flexibility inherent in skateboarding and serves to remind all skaters, whether beginner or expert, that the possibilities within this great pastime are almost limitless.

safety equipment

There are four main pieces of safety equipment used by skateboarders, and each one relates to a specific type of skateboarding. Although it is not necessary to wear every type while learning, it is still advisable that beginners invest in some safety equipment to protect them while they work out the basics.

When buying safety equipment, select reliable brands. Make sure that all padding fits securely and is held in place with adjustable straps. Your local skate store will be able to offer advice and should be happy for you to try on different products.

HELMETS

These are essential for anyone skating vert ramps or larger concrete parks, as a slam (or head bongo) at high speed can produce serious injury. There are a variety of skateboard-specific helmet brands on the market, all offering slightly different takes on the classic design. Things to look out for are: good-quality padding on the inside; a strap system that allows you to get a tight but not restrictive fit; and air holes at the top to allow heat and sweat to escape. All decent skate stores will stock a range of helmets in different sizes and styles, so consult them for advice before purchasing.

ELBOW PADS

These are a scaled-down version of the knee pad and serve a very similar function. Many safety equipment brands will offer knee and elbow pads in sets, and care should be taken to insure that your elbow pads fit snugly.

COMMON INJURIES AND HOW TO TREAT THEM

TWEAKED ANKLE

A very common and painful skateboard injury. While the pain may seem unbearable to begin with, there are several basic techniques that you can employ to help your body heal. Tweaking an ankle means that you've twisted your foot in an unnatural way and have sprained or bruised the muscles and tendons in the process. Most skaters will treat minor tweaks themselves with a combination of rest, ice, compression and elevation, or R.I.C.E as it is known. Ice is used to bring down the immediate swelling, as is elevating your foot. Compression means bandaging or supporting your injured ankle while it heals, and rest is pretty obvious.

TWEAKED WRIST

This is the wrist equivalent of the injury described before, and should be treated in the same way using the R.I.C.E. technique.

STRETCHING

Stretching and warming up before skating is the best way to avoid injury, as your muscles will be flexible and prepared for the abuse that skateboarding can sometimes mete out.

IMPORTANT

Always seek professional medical attention after any injury, as the full extent of the damage may not always be apparent immediately.

KNEE PADS

Again, these are an essential piece of kit for anyone wanting to learn how to skate larger transitions or concrete parks. They are not really appropriate for street skating. The purpose of knee pads is two-fold: not only do they protect your knees from impact, but they also allow you to knee slide out of falls. This spreads the impact and keeps you safe. As with helmets, there are many variations on the basic knee pad on the market, so consult your local skatestore for advice and sizing. Be careful that your knee pads are not too large or loosely fitting. If they are loose they can tear off while knee sliding, which can cause serious injury.

WRIST GUARDS

This is one piece of safety equipment that is applicable to all types of skateboarding. It is the one thing all beginners should consider investing in. Regardless of your level, most skateboard slams will mean that your wrists take the brunt of the impact. Broken and sprained wrists tend to be the number one injury in skateboarding.

Wrist guards work by creating a brace around your wrist, so that when you fall your hand and wrist are not bent in an unnatural way. As with every other piece of safety equipment, the variations on the basic wrist guard are virtually endless, so consult your local skate store for advice.

chapter three

tricks for beginners

You've watched all the other skaters having fun with their boards, and now it's your turn to give it a go. You've got your board fitted up, your safety gear on and now you're ready to roll. This chapter will give you the basic moves on which all the other tricks in boarding are based. It starts very gently with pushing off and tic tacking, two fundamentals that you need to practice. It then shows you how to do some slightly more difficult moves before teaching you the ollie, the trick on which almost all other moves in skateboarding are based. There are variations on the ollie too. When you can do all the moves in this chapter, you are well on your way to being a skater.

pushing off

This is one of the first and most basic moves in learning how to skateboard. Pushing off and tic tacking (pages 46–47) are essential for board control, so practice these two exercises in sequence until you feel comfortable enough to move on to the tricks.

Place your front foot toward the nose of your board with your toes pointing forward.

With your back foot flat on the ground, gently push and transfer your weight to the front foot. Do this slowly at first.

As you begin to roll, face forwards. Check your balance, and adjust your body so you feel stable. Turn your front foot until parallel with your trucks.

TIP

Don't give up, even if these beginner moves seem too difficult to master. Remember that all the great skaters—both the pros and the ones you watch at your local park—started out sometime and spent hours getting the basics right. And once they did, look what happened. Keep at it.

Bring your back foot onto your board and stand with your weight evenly balanced.

Now that you are rolling, shuffle your back foot so that it sits squarely across your tail.

As your roll slows, bring your arms down to your sides, keeping your body balanced.

tic tac / kickturn

Along with pushing off (pages 44–45), tic tacking is a basic—the foundation of all your other moves in boarding. Practice it as much as you can: it will help you to learn new tricks faster and more easily.

Stand on your board with your back foot on the tail of the board and your front foot behind the front wheels.

Raise your arms out to your sides to help you to balance, then move your front foot forward toward the nose of the board.

Stand evenly balanced on both feet, feeling the board rock beneath your feet.

Now shift most of your weight onto your back foot and the tail of the board. You will feel the nose of the board come up into the air below your front foot.

Pivot the board on your back foot so you get used to the feel of the nose and tail, as well as the weight you have to apply to move one or the other.

When all four wheels are back on the ground, shift your front foot back to the start position and stand balanced. Lower your arms.

powerslide

The powerslide can be used to slow you down and to stop your skateboard. It is the best way of slowing down (and scraping your back foot along the ground when rolling at high speed ruins your skate shoes).

Roll along at a moderate speed. Take the weight off your front wheels slightly and make the motion of a kickturn, but without lifting your wheels off the ground. You have to force your wheels to slide here, so be firm.

As you start to turn, bend your knees slightly and lean backward. The aim is to slide your wheels through 90 degrees, and then to allow your momentum to force you to skid sideways.

Lean back slightly, but not too much or you will fall. Using your outstretched arms for balance, slide forward as your wheels skid along the ground.

As you feel your slide slowing down, begin to turn your shoulders to prepare to return to a normal rolling position. You will need to transfer your weight from the sliding position so that all your body weight is centered again.

Slide your front wheels back to their original position and continue rolling at a slower speed. You will find that powerslides are much easier to do when you are traveling fast.

Roll along and prepare yourself to repeat the move with more speed. Powerslides feel incredible and, once mastered, will make you a much more competent skater. Congratulate yourself on what you have just accomplished. You now have the know-how to break your speed without ruining your shoes.

manual rolls

The manual roll, or wheelie, is a key building block for more advanced skateboard tricks. Start with manual rolls (on the back wheels), as nose manuals (on the front wheels) require more balance and board control.

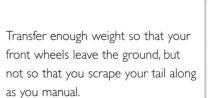

Roll along, keeping your back foot on the tail of the skateboard, and your front foot just behind the front trucks.

Visualize lifting your front wheels from the floor while rolling along. Begin to shift most of your weight to your back foot, using your front foot for control.

Transfer enough weight so that your front wheels leave the ground, but not so that you scrape your tail along as you manual.

> **TIP**
> Visualization is a great help with manuals—and lots of other moves too. It helps if you can visualize lifting your front wheels from the floor before you actually start to do it.

As your front wheels lift off the ground, stretch out your arms and use them to balance. Roll along on your back wheels with your posture holding you in manual. Enjoy the feeling of rolling balance.

As you begin to slow down, transfer your weight back toward your front foot and allow your front wheels to descend slowly.

Land with all four wheels down and make sure that your weight is centered again.

nose manuals

The nose manual requires more balance and board control than the manual roll. Raising the tail of the board using a downward force of the front foot and holding the point of balance needs a very delicate touch.

Approach the nose manual with a little less speed than for the basic manual roll. Remember that if you scrape the nose while trying to wheelie along, you will be thrown forward off your deck onto the ground.

Place your front foot in the center of the nose and your back foot on the tail. Shift your weight to your front foot without pressing the nose too heavily. As your back wheels lift off the ground, extend your arms and balance.

Lock yourself into the nose manual stance with your arms and hips. Look at the ground in front of you and concentrate on keeping your balance centered.

Enjoy the feeling for as long as you have speed; you will need to make minor adjustments to your position to maintain the balance.

As you slow down, transfer your weight back toward your rear foot and gently lower the back wheels.

Land with all four wheels down and center yourself so you stay in balance on your board.

boneless one

Along with the ollie, the boneless is usually one of the first tricks that any new skateboarder will learn. Like the no-comply, the boneless is one of only a few popular tricks that does not involve the ollie. Learn this one on flat ground and then take it to all manner of obstacles, from mini-ramps to flat banks.

Roll at a moderate speed with your back foot firmly on the tail and your front foot just behind your front truck bolts. It may help to hang your front foot off at the heel edge slightly. Prepare to execute the boneless by crouching and visualizing where you are going to plant your front foot.

Take your front foot off the board at the heel side and plant it on the floor. Reach down and grab the toe side of the board edge.

Balance on your planted foot, holding your board in your trailing hand, your back foot over the tail. Begin to lift your board upward, toward waist height, and prepare to push up off your planted foot.

Hop off your planted foot when your board reaches waist height, maintaining your hold on the edge of the board. Jump as high as possible, letting your forward momentum guide you along.

As your jump begins to peak, bend your back knee, bringing your front foot back onto the board. Hold it firmly or you won't be able to get your foot back on it. Make sure both feet are over the truck bolts.

Once both feet are back on the board and over the truck bolts, it is time to release your grab. As you do so, prepare to fall back toward the ground and concentrate on keeping your board level in the air. Land with all four wheels down and bend your knees to absorb the impact of landing.

no-comply

This, like the boneless one, is one of only a few street tricks that are not based on the ollie. The no-comply entered the skateboarder's trick vocabulary during the mid-1980s, after being popularized by Ray Barbee, a famous American professional skateboarder.

Visualize "scooping" your tail with the no-comply. Roll with your back foot across the tail's middle and your front foot just behind the front truck bolts, with your heel slightly off the edge.

Step off your board with your front foot, leaving your back foot on the tail. As your front foot plants on the ground, your board will angle upward, and you will need to control it by moving your back foot to compensate. Your board should begin to turn through 90 degrees as your front foot hits the ground.

As soon as you feel your board lift up, guide it by turning your shoulders in the direction that you want to go. As your board almost rotates 180 degrees, jump up with your front foot, and turn your body so that you are above your board and facing in the opposite direction.

Bring your board level with your back foot and jump around, placing your front foot back onto the board toward the nose. Make sure to compress the impact by bending your knees, and use your arms to balance yourself.

With both feet back on the board and placed over the truck bolts, ride away fakie. Turn your shoulders and begin to kickturn your way around so that you are facing forward again.

Ride away cleanly, and think about what to try your no-comply out on next. There are many different variations of the trick, which you will be able to tackle once you have mastered the basic technique.

ollie

This is the most important trick in skateboarding today. The ollie was invented in the early 1980s by an American skater called Alan "Ollie" Gelfand. Once you have mastered it, the potential of skateboarding really opens up and almost anything becomes possible.

Foot placement is crucial with the ollie. Place your back foot on the edge of the tail, and set your front foot just behind the front truck bolts. Practice setting your feet this way and rolling before going on to the next stage.

As you roll, begin to bend your knees and crouch down on your board. Visualize snapping your back foot and tail against the ground while jumping upward a fraction of a second later. This will help you master the timing.

Hit the tail against the ground as hard as you can with your back foot. You will have to experiment to work out the precise details of where to place your back foot, as everybody's ollie is slightly different. As soon as your tail pops off the ground, jump upward. This crucial moment in the ollie will take some practice.

As you lift upward, angle your front foot and scrape it up the board, stopping at the nose. Now tuck your back leg up while leveling the board out with your front foot. You must concentrate on keeping the board as level as possible in the air, with your feet positioned over the bolts at either end.

As you level out in the air, your ollie will peak and you will begin to fall back toward the ground. Again, focus on keeping the board as level as possible at all times.

Land with all four wheels down and bend your knees to absorb the impact of landing. Stay compressed until you are in control and balanced again and rolling forward, then you can stand upright.

shove-it

The flatland shove-it (or push-it) is another basic street trick that does not require the ollie technique. This one is quite easy to learn and is used to form the basis of many more complicated tricks that you will come across later on in your development as a skater.

Roll along with your feet set in ollie position, but with your back foot hanging off the board slightly at the toe edge. This will help you to push your board through 180 degrees while you jump above it.

Crouch and transfer your weight toward the tail, as you will make the board shove-it with your back foot. Feel the edge of the board with your toes and prepare to push down and out on the tail simultaneously, keeping enough weight on the board to stop it flying away from you.

Push the tail with your back foot and jump above it. Only land this trick if you can foresee the board turning through 180 degrees in a controlled way.

You should now be in the air above your board as it is about to complete its 180-degree rotation. Try to catch the board with your front foot when it has spun around, and is facing in the correct direction.

As your front foot lands on the deck and stops the board moving, bring your back foot onto the board and place it back on the tail. Compress and absorb the impact with your knees. Remember to balance yourself with your arms and shoulders.

Straighten your legs and stand upright again with your arms relaxed by your sides. Ride away with your eyes facing forward.

fakie ollie

The basic technique for the fakie ollie is identical to that for the regular ollie. The only difference is that this time you are rolling backward and, therefore, the timing needs to be slightly different.

Roll along backward at a moderate speed with your feet in ollie position. You may want to have your front foot slightly farther down the board to aid the fakie pop. Look straight ahead of you and visualize popping an ollie.

Crouch down as you would for a normal ollie. Pop the tail and jump upward simultaneously. You must concentrate here as the timing for a fakie ollie can be tricky at first.

As your tail pops and you begin to lift off the ground, scrape your front foot upward as you would with a regular ollie.

Tuck your back leg up while bending your knees and leveling the board out in the air with the guidance of your front foot. Make sure that both your feet are on the board squarely over the truck bolts.

As you feel your fakie ollie reach its peak, stay focused and concentrate on making a balanced landing. Keep the board under control, with the front angled.

Land with all four wheels down and compress to absorb the impact of landing. Using your arms will help you to balance and stop you from falling forward as you hit the ground. Roll away backward. Although the fakie ollie is a basic trick, it is quite difficult to get the hang of it because you are traveling fakie.

nollie

For most skaters, the nollie is their first taste of switch stance skateboarding. Learning to skate switch greatly increases your skating potential. Nollies are tricky to start with, but persevere and they will get a lot easier.

Set your feet so that they are in the position for a fakie ollie, but in the opposing stance. Let your front foot hang off the toe side of the nose, and keep your back foot in the middle of the board. Crouch and prepare to pop. You must visualize popping off the nose and immediately tucking your back leg up, similar to the fakie ollie.

Hit the nose of your board off the ground, as in any ollie-based trick. Use your back foot to control your ascent. You have to time your pop and jump perfectly here or you will not get off the ground.

As you leave the ground, use your back foot to drag the back of the board upward so that it is level with the front. This is the hardest part of the nollie. It will take some time to perfect before you pop a clean one.

You should now be at the peak of the trick, completely level in the air, with your feet flat on the griptape. Keep an eye on where you will be landing and hold your poise.

As you begin to fall back to the ground, pay close attention to keeping your weight balanced over both feet. Guide the board toward the floor and concentrate on landing with all four wheels down.

Compress and absorb the impact by bending your knees. Make sure that your feet are over the truck bolts at either end to ensure that you land safely. Straighten your legs and return to a standing position as you ride out of your compression. Roll away.

180 ollie

The 180 ollie is the next step after learning the regular ollie. As with all tricks in skateboarding, the 180 ollie can be done backside or frontside and the technique is similar for both.

Roll along at a moderate speed with your feet in ollie position. Visualize the process of popping an ollie and turning through 180 degrees. Crouch down as you would for a normal ollie and prepare to pop. Be ready to turn your shoulders as soon as you take off, so that you start to turn the first 90 degrees as you leave the ground.

Pop the tail and lift yourself up. As you take off, raise your arms upward and turn your shoulders so that your body is now at 90 degrees to your starting position.

As you reach the peak of your ollie, begin to turn the last half of your 180. You should try to land on your front wheels a fraction of a second before the back ones.

Land with both feet on the board and pivot around the last of the 180 with all four wheels on the ground.

Steady yourself with your arms and crouch to absorb the impact. Begin to stand up again as you start to roll out of the trick.

Roll away fakie. Keep practicing so that your 180 ollies are as powerful and stylish as your straight ollies.

chapter four
intermediate tricks

Now that you are more confident on your board, it's time to start getting some more interesting tricks together. None of the tricks in chapter three involved any extra gear, but that's about to change. Here we show you how to use ramps and bars in your moves. These will help you to become even more confident. In this chapter, too, are moves that get you—and your board—more airborne, with twists and flips. Take it slowly to begin with, practicing one or two moves before you start to add in more. You will soon find that tricks that looked impossible a short time ago have become part of your signature repertoire.

50-50

The 50-50 is the most basic of all the grinding tricks, which involves dragging the metal hangers of your trucks across a hard edge. The trick gets its name from the fact that both trucks are in contact with the grinding edge of the bar.

Set your feet in the ollie position and line yourself up parallel to the bar.

Crouch and pop an ollie big enough to get above the bar. You must level out your ollie before making contact with the bar so that both trucks land simultaneously into the 50-50.

Land on the bar, crouch and balance yourself as you lock into the grind. Make sure that both trucks are fully locked into position. Lean backward a little into the grind and stand up on top of it. Now you can enjoy the feeling of a controlled grind for as long as you can maintain speed.

TIP
One key element with the 50-50 is your speed of approach to the bar. Grinding requires momentum, so if you approach the bar too slowly your trucks will stop dead on the bar. Always aim to approach at a moderate speed.

Be aware of the end of the bar as you move toward it, and shuffle your feet a little so that you can pop a weak ollie as you get to the end.

Lean backward onto the tail as the front truck leaves the bar, but don't lean back too far. Make the motion of an ollie without popping the tail fully, and you should clear the end of the bar easily.

As you come out of your grind, you need to make sure that your board is level. Land with all four wheels down and bend your knees to absorb the impact of landing. Straighten your legs, relax your arms and return to a standing position as you roll away.

backside boardslide

The boardslide is generally the first block or bar trick that any skater learns. Originally, it was a trick invented by pool skaters, but it was then taken to street obstacles using the ollie. Remember that boardslides require a certain amount of speed to make the bottom of the deck slide.

Make sure that your run up is long enough so you approach the bar at a moderate speed. A short run up will not be enough. As you push toward the bar, focus on the point where you will need to ollie.

Set your feet in a regular ollie position, and use your arms to help you keep your balance. As you near the bar, crouch slightly and bend your knees. Judge your move carefully as you begin to pop your ollie.

Turn your ollie through almost 90 degrees so that you are slightly above the bar and prepare to balance yourself. Make sure that you are fully on top of the bar with your feet at either end of the deck.

Adjust your position so you distribute your weight evenly between both feet. Use your shoulders and arms to balance your slide and lean back slightly. Hold your position and slide the full length of the bar.

Pay attention to the end of the bar as you approach it. Visualize turning your shoulders and board back onto the ground. Turn your shoulders as your board clears the end of the bar. Land with all four wheels down, traveling forward.

Compress slightly to absorb the impact and slowly turn to face the front again. Straighten up into a standing position and relax your arms by your sides. Roll away, contemplating your next boardslide.

backside noseslide to fakie

The noseslide works on exactly the same principle as the boardslide; the only difference is the part of your board that you choose to slide on. As with the boardslide, you will need to approach the block at a moderate speed in order to make the noseslide.

Approach the block at a slight angle with your feet set in ollie position. Visualize the point at which you will need to pop your ollie.

Crouch down and then pop an ollie high enough so that you can get the nose completely above the block. Turn your shoulders as you pop and turn the board through 90 degrees.

While in the air above the block, push your front foot down so that the nose locks onto the edge of the block. Press your foot down hard and turn your shoulders back so that you are facing forward.

TIP

It is important to keep all movements fluid with this trick. This especially applies to the turning of your shoulders and back foot as you near the end of the block. If this movement is anything other than smooth, you will not be able to land cleanly and smoothly with all four wheels down.

Lock yourself into position and stand on top of your noseslide while guiding the slide with your back foot. Concentrate on holding your position here so that your slide is controlled.

As you get close to the end of the block, begin to turn your shoulders and back foot.

Turn through 90 degrees as you feel yourself leaving the block and land clear of it. Compress to absorb the impact of landing.

75

kickflip

The kickflip is the basic move that all other kickflip variations are based on. To be a proficient and well-rounded skater, concentrate on learning the basics before moving on to more difficult tricks. Focus on flicking the board cleanly and catching it in the air with your back foot.

Roll at a moderate speed with your feet in ollie position. You will need to angle your front foot slightly with your heel off the edge and your toes angled toward the nose. Crouch and prepare to pop the tail. You need to visualize moving your front foot up and out as you pop, flicking the board with your toes, making it flip over.

Pop the tail and flick upward and out as you feel yourself leaving the ground. You need to jump upward as well so that your body is above the board as it flips.

Flick the edge of the board with your toes and watch it flip beneath you. Stay above the board, keeping both legs level to ensure that you catch the board flat.

Watch for your griptape to reappear beneath your feet as your board completes the flip. You need to visualize catching the griptape with both your feet over the truck bolts.

Catch the board and keep it level. As you fall toward the floor, concentrate on landing with all four wheels down.

Compress and absorb the impact as you land. Use your arms to maintain your balance. Gradually stand back up on your board and relax your arms by your sides. Roll away clean, facing forward. Keep practicing this move until your pop and flick are both perfect.

heelflip

The heelflip is a close relation of the kickflip and is also the root of many more complex heelflip variations. The technique is quite similar to that of the kickflip, except the board is flipped by the front heel and rotates in a counterclockwise direction.

Roll forward with your feet in ollie position. Your front foot should be hanging off the side of your board along the toe-side edge. Make sure that your back foot is well placed to pop the tail hard.

Crouch down and prepare to pop. Visualize yourself doing an ollie and then kicking your front foot up and out to the side. This movement will pop the board into the air and start its rotation. Now try it.

Hit the tail and flick the board with your front heel while jumping above the board. Keep your arms outstretched to help you balance.

TIP
Once you have caught your board, it's important to keep it level as it falls back to the ground. The best way to do this is to use your feet for maximum control.

Stay above the board and try to keep level. Bring your front foot back toward the board as you prepare to catch it.

Catch the board as the griptape reappears beneath you. Use your feet to keep the board level as it falls back to the ground.

Compress your body to absorb the impact. Make a balanced landing, spreading your body weight evenly across both feet. Check that your feet are above the truck bolts. Straighten your legs and return to an upright position. Slow yourself to a stop with your back foot.

pop shove-it flip

Also known as the varial kickflip, this is basically a combination of the pop shove-it and the kickflip. The trick involves elements of both techniques and is a good place to start learning other kickflip variations.

Set your back foot on the tail, as for a pop shove-it, and angle your front foot into kickflip position. Roll on your board at a moderate speed. Crouch and prepare to pop the tail, scoop and flip at the same time. Visualize this process in your head as you prepare yourself.

Pop the tail while scooping it around. As your board begins to shove-it, flick your front toes out and make the board flip as it rotates.

The board should be flipping and rotating through 180 degrees beneath you at this point. Watch for your griptape to reappear.

TIP

With the pop shove-it flip, the catch is vital. You need to catch your board flat in the air so that you can get your front foot back on it easily and smoothly.

As your board completes the flip, catch it with your front foot first. You need to catch it flat in the air so that you can get your front foot back on.

With both feet placed over your truck bolts, guide your board back toward the ground and concentrate on keeping it level.

Compress to absorb the impact as you land. Straighten up into a standing position and ride away.

81

half-cab kickflip

Two separate tricks are incorporated into this variation. You will first need to break this trick down into the two elements, and then combine them into the half-cab kickflip.

Roll backward at a moderate speed with your feet set in ollie position and your front foot ready to flip your board. Crouch and prepare to pop the tail while turning 180 degrees and flipping. It helps to visualize this process before attempting it.

Pop the tail and turn your shoulders through the first 90 degrees of your half-cab. As the tail hits the ground, begin to flick the board with your front foot.

As you peak in the air, you should still be at about 90 degrees, with your board beginning to flip beneath your feet. Try to relax and flip the board in a casual but powerful manner, as this will help you to catch it.

TIP
Power, as well as a casual approach, are key to the flip in this trick. Try to relax as you flip the board in a powerful yet casual manner, as this combination will help you to catch it cleanly.

Stay above your board and wait for the griptape to reappear beneath your feet. Turn your shoulders as the board turns through the last 90 degrees.

Catch the board with your feet over the truck bolts and guide it through the last few degrees of the 180-degree turn.

Land with all four wheels on the ground and your feet steady on the board. Compress to absorb the impact. Straighten up into a standing position and relax your arms. Ride away on your board, facing forward.

fakie kickflip

This is another variation of the basic kickflip. The fakie
flip incorporates the techniques of the fakie ollie with
that of the basic kickflip. As with all fakie tricks, you will
need to master the timing, so persevere.

Roll backward at a moderate speed
with your feet in kickflip position.
Visualize the timing of popping a flip
and traveling backward.

Crouch and prepare to pop the tail,
traveling fakie while flicking your front
foot out at the same time.

Pop the tail and begin to flip your
board. Jump above your board so
that it is flipping beneath your feet
with enough room to rotate.

Stay level over the board and wait for the griptape to reappear. Prepare to catch your board and make sure that it is level.

Catch the board with both feet and guide it back down to the ground. Balance yourself, using your arms, for the backward landing.

Land with all four wheels down, compress to absorb the impact, and lean into the ground slightly. Once you are balanced, straighten your knees and stand back above the board. Roll away fakie.

ollie off ramp

Once you have mastered the flatland ollie, you can take what you have learned to a kicker ramp. Popping an ollie off of the ramp at speed will give you much more height and airtime than doing it on the flat.

Roll toward the ramp at a moderate speed with your feet in the ollie position. Now is the time to visualize the point on the ramp where you will need to pop the tail.

Crouch and prepare to ollie as you ride up onto the ramp. Stay crouched and maintain your focus as you roll up the ramp. Pop your ollie as you feel your front wheels leave the edge of the ramp. Tuck your body upward, and use your momentum to throw you up.

Guide your ollie with your feet and concentrate on leveling your board out. Stay above your board.

TIP
Visualization is the key as you approach the ramp. It is helpful to visualize the point on the ramp where you will need to pop the tail before you actually start to time your approach.

Keep level and balanced as you peak in the air; hold your position. As you begin to fall back toward the ground, keep focused and be aware of your landing point.

Land with all four wheels down and both feet on the board.

Compress to absorb the impact of the landing. Straighten out your knees and body, and stand back up on your board. Roll away.

one-footed ollie

The one-footed ollie is a relatively simple ollie variation that can be performed on all manner of obstacles. Concentrate on popping your ollie high enough so that you are able to kick your foot fully off the nose.

Roll along with your feet in ollie position. Visualize kicking your front foot off the nose of your board at the peak of your ollie. Crouch toward your board and prepare to snap your back foot and the tail against the floor.

Pop the tail and ollie as high as you can. Take your arms out to shoulder height to help you balance.

As your ollie begins to level out, continue the movement of your front foot up the board and kick it off the end of the nose. Keep your board level with your back foot while you peak in the air, with your front foot off the board.

Replace your front foot on the board as you begin to fall back toward the ground. Keep your legs bent to absorb the landing.

Concentrate on keeping the board level. Crouch and land with all four wheels down, keeping your feet over the truck bolts.

Straighten your legs and back, relax your arms by your sides, and roll away.

chapter five
advanced tricks

Now is the time to really get with the big kids, with slides, kicks, flips and grinds. This chapter shows you how to do the moves that will get you noticed, the sort of moves that are likely the reason you wanted to get into skateboarding in the first place. They're not easy, but like everything you have learned up to now, practice will make them a lot easier. In the same way as the intermediate moves built on those in the beginner chapter, so all the tricks in this chapter build on those from chapter four. Enjoy learning and practicing these thrilling moves.

frontside lipslide

Once you have learned the basic sliding and grinding tricks, you can begin working on the many variations. The lipslide is similar to the basic boardslide; the only difference is that you pop an ollie over the bar and into the slide.

Roll toward the bar at a moderate speed. Make sure that your feet are set in the ollie position. Crouch down and get ready to pop an ollie high enough to get above the bar.

Visualize landing on the middle of your board with your weight centered. Pop the tail and begin your ollie. Turn your shoulders so that your ollie turns through 90 degrees.

As you reach the 90-degree point, land on the bar. Remember to lean forward slightly, using your arms to help you keep your balance.

TIP

The more you slide, the more your confidence at sliding will grow. For this reason, when you slide, slide as far as you can. Getting a good speed as you land on the bar and leaning forward as you slide will give you the momentum to create longer, confidence-building slides.

Begin the slide, paying particular attention to remaining upright and keeping your legs as straight as possible. Allow your momentum to carry you along the bar. Maintain your slide for as long as you can.

As you reach the end of the bar, begin to turn your shoulders and hips. You need to turn your body so that you land rolling forward.

Bend your knees to absorb the impact as you land. Use your arms to balance, then slowly straighten your legs and roll away.

frontside 5-0 grind

This trick builds on the basic 50-50. Use the same techniques but lean back slightly so that you land and grind on your back truck only.

| Approach the block at a moderate speed with your feet in the ollie position. Crouch and prepare to pop your ollie while concentrating on landing cleanly on your back truck. | Pop an ollie that is high enough to take you over the block and land in the manual roll position with your back truck on the grinding edge. | Use your arms to help you balance and remember to lean back into the grind. Try not to scrape the tail, as this will hinder your grind. |

Lock yourself into the grind and allow your momentum to carry you along the bar. Maintain your balance. Keep an eye out for the end of the bar and prepare to center your weight again as you come out of the grind.

Shuffle your feet so that you clear the end of the bar, and level your board out so that you land with all four wheels down.

Bend your knees to absorb the impact as you land. Balance yourself, straighten up and then ride away.

feeble

This is another variation on the 50-50 (see page 70).
The main differences are the position of your body and
the back truck on the grinding edge. Concentrate on
locking into the feeble, which is a combination
of the 5-0 grind and the boardslide techniques.

Approach the bar at a moderate
speed and get your feet in position
on the board to pop an ollie. Crouch
as you get close to the bar and
prepare to ollie high enough to get
above the bar. You need to visualize
yourself in the feeble beforehand,
because locking into this trick can be
difficult at first.

Pop an ollie when you are parallel
with the bar so that the back truck
locks onto the bar and your front foot
is pointing down. Avoid leaning too far
either way or you will stop dead.

Your back truck should be locked
into the feeble, with your front foot
pointing toward the ground on the
other side of the bar. Lean onto your
back truck so that you begin to grind.
Use your toes to direct yourself.

Stay locked in the feeble and feel yourself grinding along the bar on your back truck. As you approach the end of the bar, visualize lifting your front foot so that you hop out of the grinding position. This part can be quite difficult until you have mastered the trick.

Guide yourself toward the ground as you feel your back truck leave the bar. Aim to keep your board level as you complete the trick so that you land with all four wheels down at the same time.

Land your board and crouch to absorb the impact. Using your arms to keep your balance, straighten up into standing position and roll away.

frontside noseslide

This is the frontside version of the basic backside noseslide. Frontside means that you will be sliding blindside, facing away from your direction of travel. Practice locking into frontside noseslide first so that you are confident with the technique before you attempt to perform the trick with speed.

Approach the block with your body facing the sliding edge and your feet in the ollie position. Visualize your point of takeoff so that you will be able to lock into noseslide.

Crouch and pop an ollie high enough for the nose of your board to be level with the block. As you pop, turn your shoulders through 90 degrees so that you are at a right angle to the block.

Land on the block and lock the nose onto the edge by putting most of your weight onto your front foot.

Once you have locked into the noseslide and have begun sliding along the block, use your front foot to hold the position. Lean into the nose and slide with as much speed as you are comfortable with. It may help to wax the edge of the block to improve your slide.

As you near the end of the block, take the weight off your front foot and turn so that you pop out of the slide and return to a forward position. It is crucial that you clear the block to avoid catching the edge and falling off.

Level your board out and prepare to land with all four wheels down, rolling forward. Land, crouch to absorb the impact and roll away.

frontside smith grind

This is another variation on the basic grinding theme. The frontside smith is similar to the 50-50 and the feeble, with most of the emphasis on the back foot throughout. Practice and you will master this trick.

Roll toward the block at a moderate speed. If you go too slowly, your back truck will stick and you will not be able to grind. Crouch and prepare to pop with your feet set in ollie position. As with all grinding tricks, your ollie needs to be high enough to get you on top of the block.

As you rise above the block, your feet need to be perfectly weighted at this stage; otherwise, you will stop dead.

Land with only your back truck locked onto the grinding edge and your front foot pointing forward and down. As you do this, shift most of your weight to your back foot so that you begin grinding.

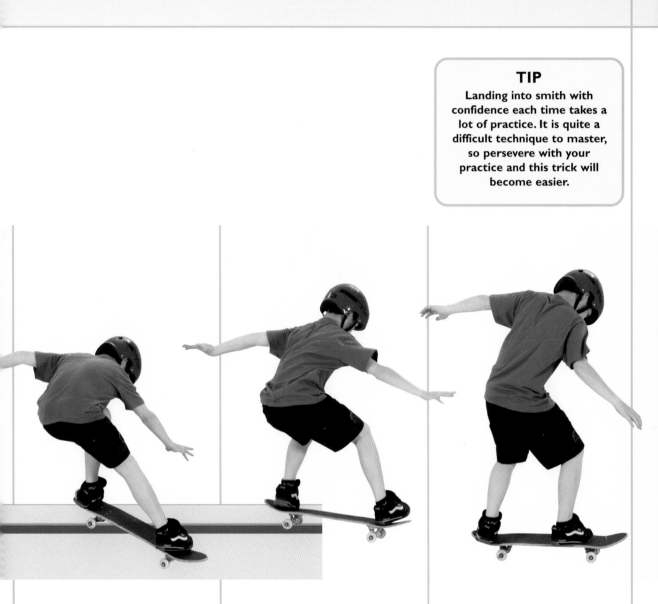

TIP
Landing into smith with confidence each time takes a lot of practice. It is quite a difficult technique to master, so persevere with your practice and this trick will become easier.

Continue pressing down on your back foot while pointing your front foot slightly downward.

Grind for as long as your speed allows. As you reach the end of the block, visualize making a weak ollie with your feet. This will lift you out of the smith grind.

As your back truck leaves the block, lift your front foot and hop out. You must concentrate on keeping the board level in the air as you do this. Land with all four wheels down at once and compress to absorb the impact. Straighten up into a standing position and ride away.

frontside nosegrind

This is another grinding variation that uses elements of both the ollie and the nose manual. Speed and balance are crucial, as it is very easy to stick while attempting to nosegrind.

Roll toward the block at a moderate to fast speed with your feet set in ollie position. Visualize grinding on your front truck while balancing. Crouch and pop an ollie keeping the point where your grind will begin in your mind's eye.

Pop an ollie and point your front foot down so that you will land with only your front truck in contact with the grinding edge. You might find it helpful at first to visualize landing into nose manual.

Land with most of your weight on your front foot and use your back foot to balance yourself. Your forward momentum should be sufficient for you to grind along the block on the front truck at a comfortable speed.

Use your arms and back leg to hold yourself in the nosegrind position and continue along the grinding edge for as long as your speed allows you to. As you get to the end, you need to decide how you are going to get off the block (see tip box above).

As you feel your back wheels clear the end of the block, begin to level your board out in preparation for landing. You must lift your front foot as you come out of the grind to keep the board level.

Land with all four wheels down and crouch to absorb the impact. Gradually straighten up into a standing position and ride away.

crooked grind

The crooked grind or crooks is a variation of a nosegrind where you sit in the grind at a slightly crooked angle to the block. As with the nosegrind, you really have to concentrate on learning how to lock your body into position for the trick.

Roll toward the block at moderate speed with your feet set in ollie position. You should be almost parallel to the block on your approach. Visualize your movements as you prepare for the trick. Crouch and pop an ollie. As with the regular nosegrind, you need to land with most of your weight on your front foot.

Land with your front truck on the grinding edge with your foot slightly weighted to the heel side. You need to lock yourself into this position, which is best described as a cross between a noseslide and a backside nosegrind.

Put most of your weight onto the front truck and use your back leg to guide your grind. Avoid leaning too far forward and use your arms to help keep you balanced. Sit in this position and allow yourself to grind for as long as possible. Keep your weight firmly on the front foot and stay balanced.

TIP

The trick here is to lock your body onto your board: it really needs to become part of your body. Think noseslide and backside nosegrind and lock your feet accordingly: your front foot should be weighted toward the heel. Keep your weight firmly on your front foot and stay balanced. As your trunk clears the end of the block, try to pop out of the grind, so that your momentum actually carries you through to the end of the movement.

As you come to the end of the block, prepare yourself to nollie out of the crooked grind. There is no need to pop a nollie—just make the movements of a nollie with your feet.

Try to pop out of the grind as your front truck clears the end of the block. Make the motion of a nollie and your momentum should do the rest. Stay level in the air.

Land on all four wheels, bending your knees. Return to a standing position and roll away.

backside tailslide

This is probably the most difficult and most rewarding of all the sliding tricks covered so far. Backside tailslides are the yardstick of board control and style. Once you have mastered them, you're on your way to being a very competent skater.

Roll toward the block at a moderate speed with your feet in ollie position. Place your back foot on the edge of the tail so that you can get adequate pop and can control the position of the tail during the ollie. Crouch and prepare yourself to pop an ollie.

You need to start your ollie as if you were going to do a backside 180 ollie. As you pop your ollie, turn your shoulders through 90 degrees, making sure that your tail is above the block. Guide your board through 90 degrees with your feet so that you are ready to lock the tail onto the block.

Land with the tail locked on the edge of the block and point the toes of your back foot to control your slide. Make sure that you are locked in and balanced.

TIP
As you prepare to pop your ollie at the start of this movement, you may find that it helps you to visualize yourself doing the ollie while you are in backslide tailslide position.

Lean back slightly to assist the slide while continuing to put most of your weight onto the tail. Use your front foot to guide your slide. Slide until you begin to lose speed.

As you reach the end of the block, turn your shoulders and hips so that you leave the block facing forward. You can hop out by doing the motion of an ollie as you release the tail.

Try to make sure that you land fully forward and balanced. Crouch to absorb the impact and keep your arms outstretched to steady yourself. Gradually straighten up into a standing position and relax your arms by your sides.

backside kickflip

This trick is a combination of the backside 180 ollie and the kickflip. Pay particular attention to the point where you catch the flip in the air, as this will determine how cleanly you land the trick.

Roll forward at a moderate speed with your feet set in the kickflip position. You might find it helpful to angle your back foot slightly to the toe side while you pop. Crouch and prepare to pop the tail. As you do this, remind yourself that you are going to turn in a backside direction.

Begin to swing your shoulders toward the backside as you start the trick. Pop the tail while flicking your front foot out to start the flip. As you do this, turn your shoulders in a backside direction so that your board turns and flips the same way.

Your board now should be midway through the flip at a 90-degree angle to your original rolling position. Try not to flip through the full 180-degree turn, as this will weaken your control over the whole move.

TIP
The key to successful backside kickflips is to practice the flip-catch-turn technique. Once you have mastered this, the trick becomes much easier to perform.

Catch the board with your feet as the griptape reappears beneath you. This is the crucial part: as you catch the board at 90 degrees, turn your shoulders to complete the 180-degree turn with your board on your feet.

Land backward with your weight balanced between both feet. You may need to slide your back wheels a little as you land to ensure that you have completed the backside 180 part of the trick.

Straighten your knees and use your arms to steady yourself. Roll backward until you feel well balanced. Kickturn around on your back wheels so that you are facing forward again.

tres flip

The tres flip is an advanced variation of the more basic pop shove-it flip shown on pages 80–81. The technique is effectively the same, except that with the tres flip your board flips while rotating through 360 degrees instead of the 180-degree rotation in the pop shove-it flip.

Roll forward at a moderate speed with your back foot on the tail and your toes slightly off the edge. Keep your front foot angled for a kickflip but placed slightly further back than for a regular kickflip.

The tres flip requires two distinct movements. Rather than popping the tail, you need to pop and scrape the tail with your toes while flipping the board with your front foot. Visualize what you want your board to do.

Hit the toe-side edge of the tail off the ground so that the tail begins its 360-degree rotation. As you hit the tail, flick with your front foot so that the board also begins to flip. Your board should start to flip while it's turning, so you need to jump high enough above it to give it enough room.

Watch for the griptape to reappear as the board completes its 360-degree spin and flip. Prepare to catch the board with your front foot first.

Catch the board with your front foot to stop it rotating or flipping any further. Guide your board to a level position with your front foot, and place your back foot back on the board.

As you drop, make sure both feet are positioned over the truck bolts and the board is level. Land cleanly with all four wheels down at once. Crouch to absorb the impact, straighten up and roll away.

nollie flip

The nollie flip is effectively a switch stance fakie flip, so it will help you to visualize this as you learn the necessary timing and technique. Concentrate on perfecting your nollies before you start working on this trick.

Roll forward with your feet in nollie position and your back foot angled slightly to assist the flip. Crouch and prepare to pop a nollie with your front foot while flipping the board with the back foot.

Make sure that you pop a decent-sized nollie, as this will help you to flip smoothly. As the nose of the board hits the ground, begin to angle your back foot. Flick the toes of your back foot along the end of your board and off to the heel side. This should kickstart your nollie flip.

Once you have flicked with your back foot, jump above your board and make sure your feet are not in its path.

TIP
Mastering the timing required for the popping part of the nollie flip will take some time, so persevere. It's definitely worth it.

Watch for the griptape to reappear beneath you and pause, ready to catch the board with your feet.

As you see your board completing the flip, catch it with your front foot first. Guide your board so that you can get your back foot on it and are level in the air.

Land with both feet over the truck bolts and all four wheels down at once. Crouch to absorb the impact and use your arms for balance. Slowly straighten your knees and stand back up on your board. Roll away victorious.

nollie heelflip

This is the heelflip variation of the nollie flip shown on the previous pages. As with the nollie flip, it may help to visualize doing a switch stance fakie heelflip in order to understand the timing needed for this trick.

Roll forward with your front foot in nollie position and your back foot just above the back truck bolts, angled for a heelflip. Remember that a clean and stylish nollie heelflip requires a popped nollie. Crouch and prepare to pop a nollie.

Visualize the process of popping, jumping and heelflipping with your back foot as you approach. Hit the nose off the ground and flick your back foot out toward the heel side edge of the tail. This should cause the board to start heelflipping beneath you.

Keep your feet wide apart at this point so that the board has plenty of space to begin flipping over.

Stay above your board and try to stay level in the air. Ideally, your board should be rotating in a controlled manner.

As you see the griptape reappear beneath you, catch the board with both feet. Try to position your feet over the truck bolts at either end. As you catch your nollie heelflip, make sure that the board remains level.

Land with all four wheels down at once, making sure that your feet are firmly over the truck bolts. Crouch to absorb the impact. Use your arms to balance yourself, and begin to straighten up into a standing position as you roll away.

indy grab

Once you have mastered your repertoire of flatland moves, you can move on to jump ramp or kicker tricks. The indy grab was invented by Duane Peters. The jump ramp gives your ollie more height and distance, so you really have the airtime to perfect and contort your grab.

Approach the jump ramp at a moderate speed with your feet in ollie position. You will need to travel much faster when skating ramps to enable you to boost yourself into the air.

Make sure that you hit the bottom of the ramp in a centered position. As you ride up the ramp, visualize the point of takeoff. Crouch down and prepare to pop an ollie. Pump up the ramp until you feel your front wheels leave the surface. As this happens, pop the tail and throw yourself upward and forward into an ollie.

Guide your ollie to its peak by using your front foot to level the board out at the highest point. As you do this, you need to bring your trailing hand down toward the toe-side edge of your board, ready to grab it.

Grab the board at the highest point of your ollie and straighten your front leg while bending your back leg. This will cause your board to poke downward at the nose and is known as "tweaking" your grab. The "tweak" must be fast and at the peak of the ollie. Release your grab as you feel yourself falling back toward the ground.

As you drop, concentrate on keeping your board level. Remember that you will need to absorb much more impact, as you will be falling from a greater height.

Land with all four wheels down at once and lean to control your landing. Stand up and ride away.

melancholy

The basic technique for the melancholy, or backside grab, is similar to that of the indy grab. Here, grab the board with your leading hand on the heel side of the board.

Roll toward the ramp at a moderate speed with your feet in ollie position. Make sure you line up your approach so that you hit the center of the ramp. Visualize your point of takeoff as you approach. As you near the start of the ramp, begin to crouch and prepare to pop an ollie.

Pop the tail as the front wheels leave the ramp. Throw your body weight into the ollie while consciously bringing your leading hand behind your front foot, so that you are ready to grab backside.

Guide your ollie to its peak using your front foot while tucking your back leg up at the same time. At the peak, grab the heel side of your board with your leading hand.

TIP
As you tweak your choly, you need to ensure that your board remains level in the air. Practice is the best way to be sure that this happens every time.

Grasp your board firmly and straighten your front leg to "tweak" your melancholy. You need to fold your back leg into your chest as you do this to ensure that your board remains level in the air.

Release your grab as you feel yourself beginning to fall back toward the ground. You must also straighten your back leg a little as you do this so you land with all four wheels down at the same time.

Land level and crouch to absorb the impact. Use your arms to help keep your balance. Straighten up into a standing position on your board once you feel stable.

tailgrab

The tailgrab involves an identical technique to the other two grabs shown on pages 116–117 and 118–119. In this variation, you need to grab the tail with your trailing hand. It will help if you try to visualize this as you approach the jump ramp.

Roll toward the ramp at a moderate speed with your feet in ollie position. Focus on your point of takeoff as you approach the ramp. Begin to crouch and prepare your ollie as you roll toward the start of the jump ramp.

Pop your ollie as your front wheels leave the surface of the ramp and launch your body weight upward. Guide your ollie to its peak with your front foot while tucking up your back foot into your chest.

It is important to avoid letting your back foot trail, or it will be much more difficult for you to grab the tail. Reach for the board and grab the tail firmly across the middle.

Tweak by straightening your front foot. Maintain your tailgrab until you feel yourself beginning to fall back to the ground. Release the tail and begin to straighten your back leg so that your board remains level in the air.

Land with all four wheels down at once, making sure that your weight is spread evenly across both feet. Crouch to absorb the impact.

Gradually straighten your knees and stand up on your board, using your upper body to balance yourself.

kickflip melancholy

This is a combination of the kickflip and ollie grab techniques covered in the previous three tricks. The emphasis is on popping a perfect flip out of the jump ramp and then catching it with your feet and leading hand simultaneously.

Approach the jump ramp at a moderate speed with your feet in kickflip position. Make sure that your line of approach takes you directly up the center of the ramp, as this trick requires perfect timing and execution of the pop and flick.

Crouch and prepare to kickflip as you near the bottom of the ramp. You must visualize popping your flip as high and as cleanly as possible to make it easier to grab your board at the peak moment of the trick.

Ride up the center of the ramp and pop the tail as your front wheels leave the surface. Flick your front foot firmly and propel yourself upward. Remember that a slow rotation of the flip will help you catch the board.

TIP
Timing and positioning are the keys to this trick. As your board begins its flip, make sure that you are hovering above it, with your leading hand in place to catch the board behind your front foot on the heel side edge.

As you see the griptape reappear beneath you, place your hand where you expect your board to be and grab. Catch the board with your feet almost simultaneously. Straighten your front leg to tweak the trick.

Release your grab as you begin to lose momentum and fall toward the ground. Pay close attention to the position of your feet and focus on keeping the board level.

Straighten your back leg a little to level the board out as you fall toward the ground. Use your upper body to center your body weight over both feet. Land on all four wheels and crouch to absorb the impact. Gradually stand upright on your board as you regain control and slow yourself to a stop by skidding the tail.

glossary

5-0 Grind—Grinding on only the back truck.

50-50 Grind—Grinding on both trucks equally.

180—A half rotation. Can mean either rotation in midair or on the board with two wheels in the air.

Acid Drop—To ride straight off a high obstacle and freefall to the ground.

Air—Ride a skateboard into the air, land it, and continue on.

Airwalk—A grab trick that refers to holding the nose with your front hand, while your legs are split as if walking.

Alley-oop—When a trick is performed in the opposite direction to travel, increasing the technical difficulty, in that the rider can only land the trick at the last minute.

Anchor Grind—A crooked grind without the back truck in the air, it is pushed down alongside the obstacle.

Axle Stall—A stall with both skateboard trucks evenly on the lip or object.

Backflip—A backwards end-over-end flip of both rider and board. Only perfomed off ramps.

Backside—The direction of a turn on an incline, meaning the backside of the body is facing the wall.

Bail—An intentional fall to avoid possible slam (crash).

Bank—Any sloped area under the angle of 90 degrees.

Barley Grind—Switch frontside 180 ollie into a frontside smith grind.

Bearings—Located inside the wheels to keep the wheels spinning so reducing the need to push as frequently.

Board—Often referred to as a ''deck,'' usually wood laminate that all the hardware is attached to.

Boardslide—To grind an object where the contact point is the underneath of the board.

Bolts—Part of a skateboard, four per truck, used to mount the deck and bottom plate, and to gauge feet position.

Bomb Drop—The rider jumps off a high obstacle holding the board, placing it under their feet in midair, and slamming down to the ground.

Boned—This is a tweak to a trick where one leg is straightened.

Boneless—Old-school flatland trick where your front foot pushes against jumping while holding the board with your back hand

Carve—Making a turn with all four wheels on the surface.

Coping—The material on the lip of a ramp used to grind, slide or bump.

Crooked Grind—Nosegrind while nose sliding at the same time.

Deck—Most decks are made from plywood and are 7.5 to 8 inches wide and 28 to 33 inches long

Drop in—To enter the ramp or obstacle from the top.

Durometer—A measurement of hardness of a skateboard wheel.

Fakie—Riding backwards.

Feeble—Grinding on the rear truck with the front truck over the top of the object you are grinding on making a railslide.

Frontside—When the turn/trick is done so that the rider's body is facing the outside arc of the trick.

Gap—The area between two riding surfaces over which ollies and other tricks are performed.

Going Big—Performing a trick high in the air, off a high obstacle, covering a lot of air

Goofy—Riding stance where the right foot is forward. (*see also* stance)

Grab—Grabbing either or both ends of the board with one or both hands.

Griptape—Sandpaper like material with glue on one side that sticks to the deck to provide a non slip surface for the rider.

Grind—A trick done on any lip or rail where the trucks or wheels come in contact on the edge of the lip

Half-pipe—A U-shaped ramp that is used for vert skating.

Hand Plant—A type of trick where one hand grabs the board while the other does a handstand on a lip or edge.

Hand Rail—Refers to the railing next to a staircase that skaters use to jump over, slide or grind.

Hang—Catching the back wheels or truck on the coping just before the board re-enters a ramp.

Hang Up—When a truck catches on an obstacle, usually causing a fall.

Hanger—The large part of the truck that contains the axle. It is also the part of the skateboard that makes contact during a grind.

Heelflip—While performing an ollie, the heel pushes down on the edge of the board causing it to flip over.

Heelside edge—The edge of the board closest to the rider's heels.

Hip—The point where a ramp or obstacle comes to a point. Tricks are done while flying over or off of it.

Indy Grab—The skateboarder grabs the toe side of the deck between their feet. Often referred to as an indy, this is the most common type of grab.

Jump Ramp—A curved ramp providing the rider with air to perform a trick. Most popular in street skating.

Kickflip—A variation on the ollie in which the skater kicks the board into a spin before landing back on it.

Kingpin—The bolt that holds the hanger and baseplate together.

Kick Turn—A method of turning where pressure is applied to the tail and the rider uses his weight to move the board in another direction.

Knee Pad—A type of protective padding worn on the knees.

Landing fakie—Landing backwards.

Lappers—A plastic cover that fastens to the rear truck protects the kingpin when grinding. It also prevents hang-ups by providing a smoother transition for the truck when it hits an obstacle.

Lid—A helmet

Line—The route that a skater chooses to take through a skatepark obstacle course.

Lip—The top edge of a half- or quarter-pipe, usually has a coping.

Liptrick—Any trick performed on the lip of an object.

Lipslide—To force the tail over the lip and slide on the surface before re-entry.

Load up—To transfer weight onto one side of the skateboard trucks.

Lock—The skateboarder catches the back trucks coming off the top of a vertical ramp and then re-enters the ramp coming down.

Manual—The skateboard equivalent of a wheelie in which the back wheels remain in contact with the ground while the front wheels are lifted.

Mongo Foot—This is where the rider pushes and brakes with their front foot.

Nollie—An ollie performed by tapping the nose of the board instead of the tail.

Nose guard—A plastic bumper used to protect the tip of a skateboard.

Noseslide—Sliding on an object with just the nose of the board.

Nosegrind—Grinding on only the front truck.

Nose Manual—More difficult to balance than the manual, the nose manual requires the rear wheels to be lifted off the ground.

Ollie—An air trick performed by kicking the tail of the board on the ground or ramp surface. Named after Alan "Ollie" Gelfend.

Pivot—A trick where the truck touches the top of the lip, or coping for just a moment before re-entry.

Quarter-pipe—Half of a half-pipe.

Rail—A grindable object such as a hand rail or the edge of a bench

Railside—A trick in which the skater slides the underside of the deck along an object, such as a curb or handrail.

Ramp Board—Large deck with firm wheels mounted onto on wide trucks for stability.

Regular—To ride with left foot forward.

Ripper—A really good and consistent skater.

Riser—A flat plastic pad that can be mounted between the trucks and the deck to reduce wheel-bite, that is when the the wheel touches the bottom of the deck when turning.

Run—The time allowed on the ramp or course during competitions.

Scrub a Wheel—To remove residue from a new wheel to ensure adhesion.

Sealed Bearing—A bearing system that keeps water and grit out.

Shove-it—Involves a variety of rotations of the board in increments of 180 degrees.

Slalom—A race in which the skater makes turns around cones placed on the race course.

Smith Grind—This trick entails grinding the back truck on an edge or rail, while the front truck hangs over the nearside of the object allowing the edge of the deck to rub the lip.

Spine ramp—An object created by placing two quarter or half-pipe's back to back.

Stance—There are two stances regular and goofy, regular is when your front foot is your left foot, and goofy is when your right foot is the front foot.

Street Boards—Shorter and narrower than ramp boards. Usually have a shorter wheelbase also.

Street Skating—The skating discipline that refers to the use of ramps, railings benches, anything you might find on a street.

Sweet—Cool or awesome.

Switch—Any trick which involves the rider landing or taking off backwards.

Switch Stance—When a skater can ride and do tricks in both regular and goofy foot.

Switchback—Used to describe turns that are around 180 degrees.

Tabletop—Ramp where there is a lead up to a flat top and a landing ramp.

Tail Guard—A plastic skid plate used to prevent wearing of the tail and can also be used as a means to stop the board.

Tailslide—Sliding on the tail of the board.

Transition—The curved part between 0 and 90 degrees.

Truck—The hardware comprised of the baseplate, hanger and axle.

Tweak—Bending or contorting the body and board during a skateboard maneuver.

Vert Ramp—A half-pipe where the steepest section of the ramp is straight down and is usually over 8 feet in height.

Vert Skating—The discpline of skating and tricks associated with vert ramps.

Wall—Any bank at or above 90 degrees.

Wheelbase—The distance between the front and back wheels.

Wheels—Usually made out of polyurethane, sometimes with a plastic core. These are mounted onto the axle with bearings in between.

Wipe Out—See bail.

Zonk—Hit the wall.

index

acknowledgments
the publishers would like to thank jake at
SLAM CITY SKATES,
16 neal's yard, London, WC2H 9DP
(www.slamcityskates.com)